THE LINEAR CHAINS
OF BODY AND SPIRIT

THE LINEAR CHAINS OF BODY AND SPIRIT

| GIUSEPPE CALLIGARIS

HEARTways PUBLISHING
WWW.GODMAN.ONE

Author: **Giuseppe Calligaris**
Title: *The Linear Chains of Body and Spirit*
Original title: *Le Catene Lineari del Corpo e dello spirito*
First Edition Doretti Printers Udine, 1928

Publisher, english 1st edition 2015:
HEARTways Publishing
This book exists in electronic and printed form.

Cover design & layout: *Yaroslav Gribachev, Stefan Strecker*
Graphics: *Giuseppe Calligaris (remastered)*
Print Production: *Createspace*

ISBN 978-3-942287-34-0

INDEX

Prof. Dr. Giuseppe CALLIGARIS

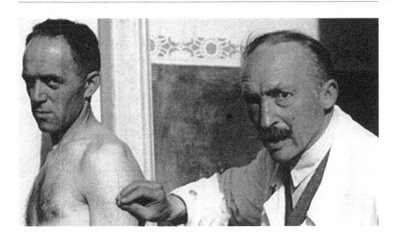

The following information is an excerpt from a lecture presented in England in 1987 by Hubert M. Schweizer from www.calligaris-akademie.de, Priest, Naturopaths, Teacher and Author.

Giuseppe Joseph Calligaris was born on October 29, 1876, in Forni di Sotto in Northern Italy, where his father was the official community doctor.

It seems that he had a calling to become a natural scientist and therapist. Calligaris studied medicine, received the highest grades and obtained his medical degree in 1901 summa cum laude at the medical facility in Bologna for his pioneering dissertation titled, *Thoughts Do Heal.*

In 1902, he went to Rome to work as an assistant to Professor Mingazzini, the director of the Institute of Neuropathology at the medical facility of the Royal University. Professor Mingazzini became his spiritual mentor for the next 25 years.

In 1909, Calligaris was asked to be the secretary of the first Italian Congress of Neuropathology. That same year he edited a

scientific book of neuropathology, and he moved to Udine, where he set up a hospital for nervous diseases together with his father.

In World War I, Calligaris had to enter the army, where he served as surgeon, and became highly honored for his outstanding knowledge and medical skills. Although he served, he was very critical of politicians and professional military people. He wrote several articles which were critical of the war and the individuals who made a profession out of it. During the war, his hospital was ruined, including his research diaries. Nevertheless, he began again, and wrote dozens of esteemed medical books and articles. Eventually he became he full professor of neurology, and lectured over a thirty year period, from 1909 through 1939.

Calligaris had no ambitions for a university career. He preferred to utilize precious time for research. He published about twenty books, comprised of approximately 20,000 pages dealing with his research into the body-mind skin-reflex chains. The majority of his materials are no longer available. After his death in 1944, they were taken by a secret division of the American government and the Soviet embassy in Bern.

Today his work forms a basis for research at twenty-three Soviet academies.

Calligaris had discovered that certain lines and points on the skin were related to the conscious and subconscious portions of the mind, and even to the enhancing of paranormal abilities. Calligaris called this new research, 'linear chains of the body-mind.' He discovered, experimentally, a network of lines – a grid of longitudinal meridians and parallels of latitude on the skin – that have less electrical resistance, are hyperaesthesic, and form geometrical patterns. For example, he discovered squares, which he called 'windows to the cosmos.'

For over thirty years, Calligaris examined thousands of individuals, and discovered that the system of coordinates and points on the skin of the human body evoked reproducible effects. He proved that everybody could be stimulated to enhance clairvoyance, clairaudience, and precognition and retrocognition, the same way that we learn writing or mathematical calculations.

Calligaris discovered points of intersections of cosmic energies which acted as mirrors, collectors and accumulators. He found that these points could be loaded [i.e. a force applied against the point], for instance, by metal cylinders, and stimulated to better reflect the higher intelligence and to produce an echo of the vital vibrations of the universe.

He believed that our brain just may be a concave mirror for the Universal Consciousness. Of course, there were many people who did not like to hear all of this, and more than once Calligaris was 'dumped' by the academic community, as well as by the Church. In 1928, he was repudiated in the Academy of Science of Udine, where he was labeled a crank. He lost his professional seat in the University, the title of medical doctor, his professional card, and the license for his hospital. He eventually developed a heart condition and diabetes, most likely due to his sorrows.

Despite all the resistance, he never lost courage in is struggle for life and the science he believed in, 'not even for five minutes,' as he himself wrote before his death. Lonely, poor, and badly affected by the second World War, he died on March 31, 1944, in Villa Magredis at Povoletto.

Today the books of Calligaris are rare. They are bought as soon as they become available, and are regarded as extremely valuable. The

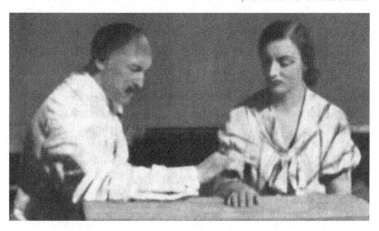

majority of his books are written in Italian, and virtually none of the works have been translated into other languages. Today, there are a few Italian academic libraries which still have some of his books, but according to government decree, they are not allowed to lend or copy them.

In several tests before professors, Dr. Calligaris took test subjects, and demonstrated that, when particular parts of the skin were stimulated, they could receive impressions which allowed them to see objects which were out of normal sight.

In order to activate the test subject to become capable of identifying objects on the other side of a wall, Professor Calligaris pressed on a particular point, located on the right side of the rib cage, for approximately fifteen minutes. Touching various points on the anatomy of the test subjects produced different capabilities.

Jules Muheim, a professor doctor of quantum physics in the Swiss Technical University of Zurich writes concerning Calligaris, *"In the future, one has to add him [Calligaris] to the greatest scientists of this century. Calligaris found that, with continuous, tender pressure on several spots of the human body . . . that not only the familiar physical feelings such as warmth/cold, tickling, itching, salivation, aches, and other sensations were generated, but emotional feelings including distortion of time and local-moving (space) within cosmic dimensions became possible.*

The grid on the body that Calligaris found corresponds to the degrees of longitude or latitude of the earth. Located on this grid are the sensitive circular areas, like islands; areas with a radius of a few millimeters, as well as other geometric forms which stimulate other cognitive abilities."

The Calligaris technique is used for the diagnosis of radiations of the mineral, vegetable, animal and human realms. Biological organisms can be trained to receive, register, and respond to these radiations through coding and decoding information in the body.

The therapeutic aspect of the Calligaris material is from the manipulation of registered radiations from disharmonious levels to harmonious ones.

The basis of the Calligaris technique is simple and easy to explain: Biological systems send out measurable radiations. These radiations give information about harmony or disharmony from the eminating organic system. This may register as sickness or health.

Of course, there are overlaps between the acupuncture system or meridians, and the lines and points of Calligaris. This is to be expected, considering that there are several thousand Calligaris points and approximately 800 acupuncture points.

Some key points of the Calligaris technique include: The human body contains thousands of spots. These spots are connected with lines, and they appear as if they were centered in the network of lines. These spots are easy to find on the human skin. The Calligaris spots are found by simply measuring the coolest spots or those of the greatest electrical conductivity. These spots have a diameter of between 8 – 12 millimeters and can be verified by relating to two or three other reflexes, which must be felt in order to make sure that the sensitizing procedure was correct.

Dr. Calligaris found that a mental image, the thought-form itself, will cause stimulation within the body. This leads to the basic idea of his doctoral thesis, "Thoughts Do Heal." There is a mental-dermal effect which physically registers on the body and shows the radiation of the thought-forms or thought-waves. Research has shown that thoughts can be regarded as objects with physical existence. Various Calligaris locations are related with certain organs, and these spots respond and correspond to emotions. So, thoughts can cause emotions and touch organs, which in turn relate to the points on the skin.

Calligaris found that the dermo-visceral-psychological-mental reflex is produced by simply rubbing certain skin areas. Resonance Diagnosis: For good results, a therapist must be well trained and in good mental and physical condition. Stimulation of the Calligaris points takes about ten to twenty minutes, depending on the case. The stimulation itself is provided by cold metal cylinders, the therapist's fingers, or by a low electrical current. Following the stimulation, the desired effects will be felt by the patient.

The following is written by Prof. Calligaris himself

THE LINEAR CHAINS
OF BODY AND SPIRIT

In 1908, I made an announcement to the Medical Academy of Rome on the subject of *Spinal sensitivity metamerism* (though it might be more accurate to call it *cerebral,* rather than spinal), explaining that human skin is intersected, across its entire surface, by special lines running in four directions: longitudinal, transversal, right-oblique and left-oblique.

The longitudinal lines, I stated, were parallel to each other and spaced, in the adult human, approximately 1 cm apart, with the exception of particular areas (neck, wrists, etc.) in which they ran closer. I pointed out the lines' perpendicular descent from the head, ranging in every direction: along the neck, shoulders and upper limbs, reaching the tips of the fingers, and along torso and lower limbs to the tips of the toes, on both front and rear as well as each side. In fact, I added, the front lines of the body are a direct continuation of the rear, as the right-side are of the left-side.

The transversal lines run in circles encircling the head, neck, torso and limbs to the very tips of the fingers, and are evenly spaced approximately 1 cm from one another, just like the aforementioned longitudinal lines, which they intersect at a 90° angle, forming a grid of 10 mm squares.

The oblique lines serve as diagonals of each single square.

Each of these squares, which I called *fundamental* (FIG. 1), delineated by two longitudinal and two transversal lines (1st Order lines), is in turn subdivided by other longitudinal and transversal lines (2nd Order lines) into as many tiny secondary squares, whose diagonals are aligned with those of neighbouring squares.

That said, I theorized that all objective sensibility disorders (central and peripheral, organic and functional) should be considered in the context of this regular grid enveloping the surface of the human body.

Following my statements, which had the air of being a revelation and a discovery rather than a theory or doctrine, the President of the Academy, Guido Baccelli – man of genius as he was – named a Commission charged with reviewing the facts I had announced.

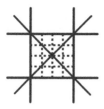

Fig. 1
A small fundamental square
(1908).

After a short time, the said Commission submitted its response to the self-same Academy, declaring that this new linear system could not be traced and advising the researcher to further continue his studies, focusing on determining the phenomena. To tell the truth, in those early days my research was still in in a chaotic, embryonic phase, leading me to glimpse much more than I could truly see and thus to state more than I could truly prove. It was no wonder, then, that the panel of experts could not at the time have a clear grasp of the facts, for I was still unable to provide solid evidence to present for their evaluation.

From then on, I never ceased pondering in my mind this great problem, which for twenty years was the main focus of my inner life as a researcher and the flame that, in silence and meditation, warmed my hungry spirit, greedy for knowledge and new scientific truths.

I continued my research, armed with patience and perseverance I can't help but be proud of today.

Only the war brought a hiatus to my obstinate fixation as an unsatisfied scrutineer; but the mysteries of the Hyperesthetic Lines of the Body were never far from my mind, oftentimes constituting the focus of my conscience, even in the midst of the tragic events and woes of the European conflict.

It seemed for a time that the invasion of Friuli would be a deathblow to my studies, a good amount of precious research material having already vanished before the rest of my papers and notes on the subject were lost, to my great sorrow.

I did not give in to circumstance, nor falter in the face of difficulty: I drew together again the infinitely complicated threads of the mysterious network and took up my studies again with calm resignation and serene faith.

Between 1908 and 1927, I published 6 series of experimental studies (the 7th and 8th studies are ready for printing), and 20 clinical works on the subject.

But I wouldn't be here to talk about it, if in recent months my investigations had not yielded, quite suddenly, the most surprising of revelations. I was therefore correct when, in 1913, in light of one of my first series of studies, I wrote the following words: «*Crescunt disciplinae lentetardeque*».

The statements I'm about to make are of such entity and importance, I feel I must free myself of them as soon as possible, like a man living an errant lifestyle and tormented by the need to take a load off his shoulders after many long years, or caught in the anguish of a tumultuous life and desperate to take a weight off his chest that had been burdening him for a very, very long time.

And before we begin, I must warn you. Because the facts I will present to you, briefly summarized, are entirely new, indubitably wonderful and an incalculably important contribution to science, I would beg you to receive them serenely and judge them prudently, allowing me for the moment not merely the mitigating circumstance of my infirmity, but also recognition of my intellectual integrity. You have not only the right, but also the duty, to make all possible reservations, until such a time as these facts shall have undergone review and been submitted to the consideration and experimentation of fellow researchers.

I start now by briefly reminding you of the results of my first studies (between 1908 and 1926). I cannot enter into detailed explanations now, but must proceed with great strides, expressing myself mainly in laconic terms and unambiguous statements.

The 5 fingers of the hand are longitudinally marked and precisely bisected by 5 median, or axial, lines. Between and parallel to these run 4 interdigital lines: the 1st, 2nd, 3rd and 4th. These 9 lines run up the arm, moving a little closer or further from one another depending on the volume of each segment, and continue on to their corresponding course on the rearward face.

Finally, it is necessary to add one last line to our scrutiny: the limb's lateral line *(lateral line of the body)*, the longest of all, running continuously on both the left and right sides and along the lateral sides of the fingers, without breaks (FIG.2).

Thus, the upper limb, hanging down by the torso, appears as one long segment, or metamer, marked by 11 longitudinal lines, which I have already named 1st Order lines: the 5 axial lines of the fingers, 4 interdigital lines, 2 lateral lines, referred to in my notes as intermediate lines.

Please now be advised that this precise longitudinal arrangement repeats itself uninterruptedly along the entire length and on all faces of the body.

FIG.2
LATERAL LINE OF THE BODY (1912)
(MENTAL DISSOCIATION–
SCHIZOPHRENIA – 1928).

The median line of the 3rd finger is quite simply a segment of the median line of the limb, also known as Sherrington's axial line, which finds its counterpart in the median line of the lower limb and of the body. I call every one of these lines *median lines*.

The *longitudinal-type* linear systems border great *longitudinal segments,* and are intersected by corresponding transversal-type linear systems bordering, in turn, *great transversal segments* (FIG. 3).

Each *intermediate longitudinal* line is intersected by many intermediate transversal lines, encircling the body like rings. They are arranged on horizontal planes, parallel to one another, each line spaced about 10 cm apart, from head to foot, drawing slightly closer or farther away depending on the volume of the various bodily segments. These few longitudinal lines, intersecting with the far more numerous corresponding and equivalent transversal lines, form a single large system: *the great intermediate system of the body* (FIG. 3).

Likewise, *all longitudinal medians* intersect with a large number of transversal medians that, like the former, circle the different parts of the body at the same distance as mentioned above for the intermediate lines: approximately 8-10 cm. The interweaving of the *few longitudinal median lines,* of which there are 5, with all these *corresponding and equivalent* transversal lines gives shape to a second system: *the great median system of the body* (FIG. 3).

At this point, you would do well to memorize this first fundamental notion, contemplating *the serial repetition of longitudinal and transversal metameres,* which says it all. You should be aware that each great longitudinal or transversal segment of the body is present uninterruptedly on the body surface, with all its attributes and its precise, pre-determined functional organization.

Let us proceed. The 11 *primary or 1st order* hyperesthetic lines, which, as we have found, are part of every great system and every great longitudinal median or intermediate segment (such as, for instance, that of the upper limbs), can also be found in every great system or great transversal segment.

Such are the facts, allowing us to move from the complex to the simple, to circumscribe the problem and to reduce the issue to a minimum by stating that each square formed by the overlap of the two intermediate linear systems, i.e. *each great intermediate square* (FIG. 4), which I call fundamentals, like the aforementioned smaller ones, as well as each square formed by the overlap of the two median linear systems, i.e. each *great fundamental median square,* actually encompass all the systems, encapsulating their structure – to put

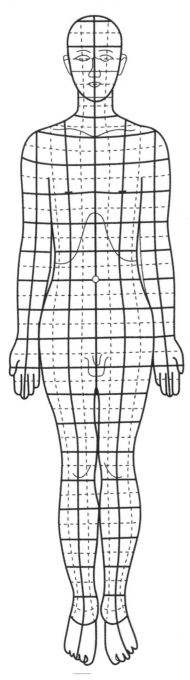

FIG. 3
THE TWO MAIN LINEAR SYSTEMS
(1924): MEDIAN OR MENTALLY
ASSOCIATIVE AND INTERMEDIATE
OR MENTALLY DISSOCIATIVE (1928).

(SEE ALSO LINES NO. 6 AND NO.1
IN FIG. 4).

it simply, they incorporate the entire body, in such a way that all that is wonderful and mysterious about the prearranged gears and mechanism of the *"linear chains of the body"* can be found – listen carefully, gentlemen – *in just one of these single great fundamental square of our body, be it median or intermediate.* Being the laws of linear conjuncture and connection well-known in only one of these squares I mentioned; being the prearranged metameric matches well-known, with their synesthetic affinities, short- and long-distance synkinetic correlations, not to mention their predetermined repercussion, as we shall shortly see, by a fixed rule and with unfailing precision in world of psyche, our eyes are opened to numerous secrets of psycho-somatic correlations, and we shall have lifted the veil on this metameric ancestral web, hugely complex and occult, whose Daedalic labyrinths I have wandered for twenty years, with no Ariadne's thread to guide me.

But I will now attempt to enlighten you on these connections, in just a few short words.

We have here a *great intermediate fundamental square* (FIG. 4). Besides its 4 peripheral sides, you can see it is crossed, longitudinally and transversally, by 9 hyperesthetic 1st order lines that, intersecting, form as many small fundamental squares. Well, imagine this great square traced, for instance, upon the anterior or ventral side of the right forearm: the 9 longitudinal lines, stretching downwards, are a realistic representation of the 5 axials of the fingers and the 4 interdigital lines I mentioned before, placed in alternating order, whilst the external ones, indicated by dashed lines in the figure, represent the two segments (internal and external) of the *intermediate or lateral line of the body* (FIG.2).

Let me say straight away that each of these 9 longitudinal lines has an *equivalent counterpart* among the 9 transversal lines bearing the same number, and I will also add that intimate contact, or as I call it, the *conjunction* of each pair of corresponding lines (one longitudinal, the other transversal) occurs, in our case, which is to say that of great intermediate squares, which are commonly found on the anterior face of the body, along the right-side (for the observer) or diagonal of the square itself. As this diagonal is a *homogeneous meeting point,* the other, that is the left-hand diagonal, is a *heterogeneous* meeting point.

We find ourselves, therefore, contemplating a great intermediate square, marked into the anterior face of the right-side forearm of an individual. Meanwhile, I warn you explicitly that the excite-

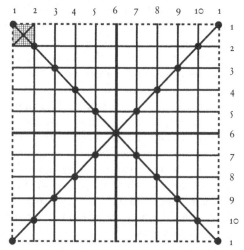

FIG. 4

A GREAT, INTERMEDIATE, FUNDAMENTAL SQUARE, WITH ITS SYSTEM
OF PRIMARY, HYPERESTHETIC LINES, LONGITUDINAL AND TRANSVERSAL,
CORRESPONDING NUMERICALLY, AND A SMALL SQUARE WITH ITS ANALOGOUS
SYSTEM OF SECONDARY LINES (1928).

ment (localized, electrical, mechanical etc.) of any pair of corresponding longitudinal and transversal lines, by which I mean that they meet on the square's right-side diagonal, at the points indicated in FIG. 4, elicits on the entire surface of the body, from head to foot, concurring echoes, precise similarities, perfect consonances in the fields of sensitivity and mobility. What's more, having already stated that the entire surface of the cutaneous tegument is nothing more than an aggregate of figures and mechanisms identical to those of the *great intermediate square,* you won't be surprised to learn that these effects take place in accordance with a geometric rule and are governed by fixed laws. It follows that by stimulating, for instance, a particular hyperesthetic line in the hand or foot, the researcher, having prior knowledge in the field at issue, can tell beforehand exactly which spots will quiver in the individual's face, for instance.

To avoid repeating myself, in a moment I will briefly explain the nature and whereabouts, for each pair of corresponding hyperesthetic lines on the body, of these repercussions, reminding you of the simultaneous representations in the world of the spirit.

However, before leading you into this new temple of wonders, let me invite you to linger a moment, so that I may furnish you with some details about the process of initiation to these profound mysteries.

It is advisable to experiment, the first few times at least, on sensitive, delicate, erethismic individuals. Some sick and convalescent people (neurasthenics suffering from epidemic encephalitis make excellent subjects) lend themselves better to this purpose than the healthy and strong. The latter will serve, should they be in a state of slight dejection or exhaustion. It seems to me that young women, intelligent and somewhat neurotic, are better suited to the purpose than men. By this, I don't mean to imply these phenomena to be the exclusive domain of certain psychotic, hysterical and highly impressionable individuals. It is more a matter of general rules of psychology and human physiology, which all humans obey to varying degrees.

Sceptics should, for instance, undergo the charging of the 1st interdigital line (running upon its correct course along the inner margin of the thenar eminence) for 30-40 minutes, and then say how clear their memory, or various memories are. And those who, to this day, still insist on ascribing these wondrous spectacles of biology down to mere suggestion, should know that the phenomena I concern myself with are, as agreed by the brightest among of the subjects I have examined, not fostered nor facilitated, but rather hindered by suggestion, and are at their most genuine when involuntary and automatic.

My experience to date has taught me the following: the examinee must be in a state of perfect calm, both of spirit and body. They must be without impression, prejudice or worry of any kind. A slight mental torpor, akin to apathy, a general oblivion and a serene indifference to the outside world are conditions favourable to the investigation. An intense flow of ideas, and physical or mental fatigue are, on the contrary, unfavourable. After physical strain, long arguments and emotional turmoil, the phenomena do not manifest. With great difficulty, it is possible to trigger them even after meals, during headaches, on windy days etc., but easy to accomplish during a woman's menstruation (though not on the days leading up to it), changes in the weather, certain lunar phases (waning moon?) and so forth. The hours preceding sleep and following awakening are, to my knowledge, the best suited to investigation, which must always be carried out in silence, isolation and meditation, far from blinding light and deafening sounds, in the presence of the researcher alone, and with little discussion. It is not only possible, but easy, to practice self-research, through which the subject, if attentive and bright, led by his own experience, learns to pick the right moment to mechanically activate all the scenarios in the secret theatre of his sub-conscious.

With these tips, research becomes very easy and within the grasp of everyone. Particular methods or knowledge of linear webs aren't necessary. All that is needed is patience on the part of the researcher, and more especially of the examinee, who must be comfortably seated (the arms should not be compressed back), holding one hand out, supported, for the researcher's scrutiny. As the latter prepares to tackle one of the 10 lines, they should not forget that the course of the lines always runs in the exact middle of the two sides of each finger, the front and the rear, and in the exact middle of each interdigital space. Only the lateral line of the body, running along its interdigital course, passes exactly between the two lateral sides, right and left, of every single finger.

Because these lines follow the same route and have the same functional meaning on both the front and rear faces of the segment of the limb being examined, they can be set upon in any point; but I usually favour the palmar face, as I believe it to be the more sensitive. And in fact, the more sensitive the cutaneous surface being explored, the quicker the onslaught of the phenomena. The fingertips (the index being particularly sensitive), like the interdigital folds, I believe represent the preferable option. If one wishes to investigate the opposite face of the finger, its median line (rear segment) should preferably be struck close to the nail. Examination of hyperesthetic skin scarring may yield more obvious results, and I can safely say that, in the case of post-encephalitic pseudo-neurasthenics, the phenomena is quicker to manifest if investigations are carried out on the side (right or left) exhibiting the hemi-syndrome.

To excite, irritate, or as I am wont to say, "charge" the targeted hyperesthetic line, we can recur to two thin metal wires (the extremities of common rheophores), or a thin bipolar electrode, injected with a mild Faradic current. Lately, however, I have taken to simpler, more practical methods. So simple and practical that psychologists and physiologists don't have them catalogued in their laboratories. It's a mistake to believe that the examination of these hyperesthetic lines, still special and mysterious in their essence, can only be carried out through the more common methods, with the use of aesthesiometers and classic algometers. We often expect to dictate laws even to phenomena we don't understand, and crucify mediums, for instance, who cannot perform upon command under the vivid light of day.

I myself use a narrow metal point, or a thin sliver of tortoiseshell, sharpened almost to a point, and use them to rub the skin lightly, several times, moving here and there (at medium velocity, meaning 60-90 rubs per minute) across an area of approximately 1 cm, making sure to keep the line under examination in the centre, so its course can be seen. In recent months, to reduce the process to a minimum, I have employed the tip of a fingernail (fingernail test), particularly useful, in self-research, as a scratching stimulus, which should remain very light, for pain hinders the manifestation of phenomena. It's important however to avoid letting the tip of the exploring finger adhere to the examined finger, for in such an event the researcher would not only charge a certain median longitudinal line in his unmoving index finger – the line corresponding to memory, for instance – but also the apical finger segment of the lateral line of the body running along the stimulating finger. In such a way, the flow of thoughts is dispersed and memory dissociated, thus hindering the phenomena.

I must confess that the excitement of a longitudinal line on the hand, when practiced upon a length of around 1 cm, as I am wont to do, has the disadvantage of also slightly charging transversal lines, holders of who knows what mysterious phenomena, which manifests and mingles together with the sought effect, muddling it. But for the moment, we must disregard these details and limit ourselves to developing a broad view of this new world, in all of its complexity.

On the other hand, it's true that another trait of these particular hyperesthetic lines is that transversal lines are excited by charges applied to the skin in a vertical direction, whilst strokes best-suited to longitudinal lines must intersect the latter at a right angle, working in a transversal direction. Thus it clear how necessary it is, for the purpose of exciting the axials or interdigital lines of the fingers, i.e. lines of the longitudinal type, that mobile stimulation, in this case scratching, be applied sideways, in the opposite direction to the lines themselves. If the longitudinal lines were to be exposed to scratching stimuli in longitudinal or oblique direction, they would not respond, or would respond weakly. Later, when we move on to 2nd order lines, these methods of scratching and stroking shall be replaced with localized excitement repeatedly applied to a single spot.

As a general rule, the various somatic phenomena that we will shortly examine, each with its own particular line, or rather its particular pair of "corresponding" lines (phenomena of the eye, of the teeth, of the lips etc.) [1], manifest after a time-lapse of between 15 and 30 minutes, while those I will now discuss generally manifest 3-5 minutes later, and their execution – regardless of individual variation - remains incomplete for at least 20-30 more minutes, or longer. The first appearance is particularly belated and the first exam especially tricky: but once the door has been opened and the subject enlightened (not conditioned!), the latency period shortens and results are ever clearer during subsequent experiences. It must not be forgotten, however, that these phenomena are weak and often even ephemeral, making it easy for them to pass unnoticed at first.

I cannot yet say what peaks might be attained by each phenomenon if the charge were to be prolonged for an hour or two, but I would assume that in a few particular cases involving special lines (those of oblivion and emotion, for instance), unpleasant consequences are indeed possible. I would warn that, after a half-hour, many subjects requested the experiment be suspended, due to causes of various nature (headaches, mental confusion, profound fatigue, tachycardia, anxiety etc.).

It is therefore advisable, should it not be the researcher's intention to study the after-effects, sometimes lasting several hours, to restore the balance of the ailing examinee by charging the antagonist line, which I will indicate in each instance. Indeed, in the application of this sure-fire remedy *(contraria contrariis curantur)*, the researcher will receive the satisfaction of a definite confirmation.

Another finding the researcher will come across derives from the comparison, following several attempts, of the notes regarding the complaints and statements (which must be brief and precise) made by the different subjects exposed to the experience; statements that the researcher himself must collect, recording them on separate sheets, as I usually do.

From these comparisons, as I was saying, they will learn that a given phenomenon always manifests with a special cortege, always arranged more or less in a particular order, as though it involved the same mantra, sparked by mechanisms repeatedly invoked in exactly the same way. The phrases uttered by examinees, their words, their facial expressions, their sensations repeat themselves almost stereotypically, one dare say almost identically, were it not for individual differences. You will in fact notice that the principal symptoms remain fixed, while a few details or aspects of the phenomena may vary. In other words, each person expresses their hate, pain or pleasure in their own personal, habitual manner.

As regards the dream experiment I should mention that my advice would be to practice self-research for 5-10-15 minutes immediately before going to sleep. In addition, to better guarantee and intensify the phenomena, the examinee should be asked to subject the line in question to brief charges, repeatedly, during the course of the day. In this way, occasionally a single electrical or mechanical charge applied during the course of the day may be enough, if sufficiently prolonged, to direct the nocturnal dream.

Let me end by saying that, in order to make the phenomena more certain during both sleep and wakefulness, occasionally it is possible to proceed with the simultaneous (or alternating) charge of the two corresponding lines of the hands or of the feet, which you should know have the same functional value. We shall later see how every somatic phenomenon manifests more vividly, and every mental phenomenon more emphatic, if we charge the meeting point of each linear system and the median line of the body, which combines and associates the functions of the two hemi-bodies.

One should not insist on the investigation by charging lines of different meaning in quick succession, as this would cause the phenomena to blend together. The fact remains that if this uneven charge is done before sleep, the resulting dream will, in most cases, be a compound made up of elements pertaining to the functions of both lines: elements easy to recognize and distinguish. But, as a general rule, the last line to be excited will confer upon the dream its own particular hue.

And now, before we begin exploring the territory, unknown to you until today, of these specific mental reactions, know that, for the purpose of avoiding repetition, each of the ten short chapters summarizing the psychic phenomena related to their respective linear chains (of which we shall consider only the longitudinal components present in a hand, as shown in FIG. 5), will include the performance, or rather the outline, of 9 fundamental topics or key themes, in this order:

1. The first physical symptom.
2. The prelude to the spirit.
3. The gradual unfolding of the mental representation.
4. The corresponding physiognomic picture.
5. The after-effects.
6. The antagonistic currents and appropriate psychological care.
7. The revelatory dream.
8. Relations with Neuropsychiatry.
9. The unconscious revelation of personality.

THE LINEAR CHAIN OF LOVE
(MEDIAN LINE OF THE THUMB)

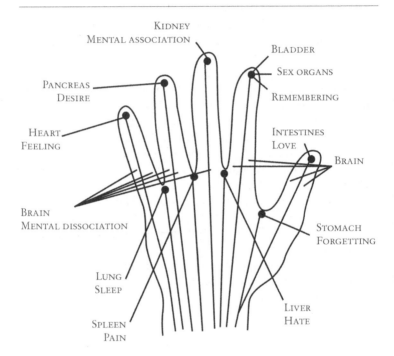

KIDNEY
MENTAL ASSOCIATION

BLADDER

SEX ORGANS

PANCREAS
DESIRE

REMEMBERING

HEART
FEELING

INTESTINES
LOVE

BRAIN

BRAIN
MENTAL DISSOCIATION

STOMACH
FORGETTING

LUNG
SLEEP

LIVER
HATE

SPLEEN
PAIN

1. The first strike of Cupid's arrow gives the victim the instantaneous feeling of a slight touch on the bottom lip when the median line of the thumb is hit (lower lip phenomenon).

2. The subject feels the sensation of the eyes widening, the lips puckering and then kissing, or sometimes the feeling of being suddenly kissed and called by name.

3. They express a desire for affectionate words, kisses, hugs, caresses, as well as their instinctive attraction toward a person. Smiles, a sense of contentment and goodwill. Love songs whisper in their ears, erotic visions of Eros make them blush with Dionysian images and, often urgently and accompanied by a slight sense

of anxiety, sexual desire then presents it self. The need sometimes arises to grasp a hand, cry and kneel before an idol, lips trembling and muttering incoherently.

4. Protrusion of the eyeballs, a tendency to pucker the lips and lean head and arms forward.

5. Brief periods of amorous glee.

6. The effects of this charge are quickly neutralized by exciting the 2nd interdigital line (line of hate), which is its antithesis.

7. Dreams of love.

8. See under mental illnesses, erotic delirium etc.

9. In the case of a subject who is frigid, charging this line will yield weak, incomplete results, arousing only pallid, uncertain sexual images. Should the subject be highly erotic, the mental representation will take place with little delay, illuminated by bright lights and clearly showing its unequivocal colours.

THE LINEAR CHAIN OF OBLIVION
(Interdigital)

1. Fleeting binding sensation or feeling of a light touch or pain in the teeth of the lower jaw when the line is charged *(lower dental phenomena)*.

2. It seems to the examinee that their body, but especially the head, tilts toward the side being tested. Soon after, vision becomes mildly blurred and the head feels heavy or constricted. In addition, dizziness occurs, as may a sense of nausea or disgust, accompanied by excess salivation and bitter taste in the mouth, an urge to vomit, sweat, shortness of breath, palpitations and general discomfort: in short, a state resembling Mènière's disease or sea-sickness.

3. Feeling of empty-headedness, inability to pin down wandering thoughts, increasing mindlessness; physical and mental asthenia, sense of powerlessness, a need of rest and desire for oblivion and surrender, holding one's head in one's hands or folding the arms; tendency to fainting, amnesia. The subjects slowly lose their memory and claim to be unable to remember because incapable of channelling and focusing their thoughts, to be restless, languid, volatile. Serious bradypsychia, yet also a feeling of great anguish for their condition. As the experiment continues, the difficulty in speaking and thinking increases, the examinee feels the need to open the eyes wide, as though to prevent themselves losing sight of a vanishing world; they are disoriented in space and time, progressively losing all memories (visual, auditory etc.). They cannot remember where they were yesterday and can recall their activities of the current day only in bits and pieces. They forget the names and faces of their nearest and dearest; cannot recognize their own mother, but for a single familiar feature; have a fragmented view of buildings, streets, squares and landscapes, with large, roughly geometrical gaps consisting

of grey bands. «I get the impression» a clever young woman stated, «that my mind is a mosaic with many pieces missing» Our subject has forgotten names, dates, the tune of popular songs, the sound of their favourite music; they could not say what they had for lunch or which road leads to home. They even lose memory of the sensitivities of their own body, which feels numb, incapable of movement, «as though dead»; they experience a bizarre sensation of having never lived, as they move towards unconsciousness and plunge into an abyss of oblivion.

4. The examinee becomes convinced their face looks stupid, their confusion is clearly visible to the researcher. The head is protruding, the mouth gaping and the eyes wide open, glassy, as though lost in the emptiness of their inner life.

5. Mild nausea or dizziness, accompanied by grogginess, mental sluggishness and memory loss; asthenia, and unpleasant sensations lasting many hours.

6. The aftereffects of the charge of this linear chain, which are among the more serious and long-lasting due to causing disturbances (often quite remarkable) of the spirit that cloud and disorient it, and over time bring on a frightening sensation of doom and impending death, are neutralized by the charge of its antipode, the median or axial line of the index (line of memory).

7. Nauseating, dizzying or lateropulsive sensations may arise during the oneiric state, as well as disorientation, terrifying, strange or paradoxical visions; situations without rhyme or reason arise in this world of dementia *(oneiric dementia)*.

8. This is the nervous chain of demential and amnesiac states.

9. Examining it may give us new information about the tendency to forgetfulness and to losing one's mind.

THE LINEAR CHAIN OF MEMORY
(MEDIAN LINE OF THE INDEX FINGER)

1. The first physical symptom is the sensation of a light touch on the inside of the mouth, in line with the point where lower lips and gums meet *(lower labial-gingival phenomenon)*.

2. At first, the electrical (bipolar method) or, even better, mechanical (fingernail test) charging of this linear chain, containing the secrets of every kind of magic, the mysteries of renewal and the most ancient relics of miracles, conducts the examinee, who is the temple of my faith and the stage showcasing these wonders, to vague recollections of places and pale memories of people emerging from a cloudy, dreamlike world. This is Mnemosyne's first, life-giving breath from the tomb of memory.

3. The marvellous phenomenon of the disinterment of childhood memories and reliving of the remotest days of one's life occurs in three stages:

1) After a period of time charging, shorter or longer depending on the individual and several factors we have already covered, a split-second occurs during which the examinee's mind goes blank, and for a moment they are seemingly in a daze.

2) Quite suddenly the memory surfaces, with the living picture of its images.

3) There follows a moment of mild mental fatigue.

Distant memories and insignificant events, the recollections of a world believed lost without trace, appear now like phantoms, peering through the windows of the past we'd thought forever closed.

The distinct memory of a door handle or of colourful floor-tiles; an iron bed-frame or a light-yellow dress with red flowers; a plaster ornament or a leather armchair; a man's head resting on the pebbles of a dry riverbed, or the bald head of another dappled by a ray of sunlight, are all fragments of memories and minuscule slivers of the past, appearing in our memories and usually requiring confirmation from family members before it can be recognized, identified and placed in space and time.

A landscape shrouded in mist on a gloomy autumn day; a wagon sitting in a field and the sound of a farmer herding his cattle; a dog running past with a rag in its jaws as a man calls its name; a large black cat sitting on a pile of wood; these are all echoes of a distant past and of the ghosts of the adult mind, reminding us of a handful of seconds of our life as 4 or 5-year-olds. A person might suddenly remember a French prayer they used to recite in childhood, from the first word to the last, though it had long since vanished into the shadows of oblivion; another might remember beating a stick against a chair whilst singing loudly, when they were 5 years old; a third will recall sliding across ice, as they did in the good old days, and a playmate shouting "the water's coming, the water's coming!" A woman observes a black canvas bag holding schoolbooks and remembers how she hated the feel of its cold metal handle when she was a girl; and another, returning to the Venice Lido after 30 years, can picture the sunlight spilling through the slats of the bathhouse, works up an appetite looking at a sandwich, remembers the cold feeling of wet blankets and smells the salty tang of the sea.

Following these examples taken at random from my notes, let us move on to observing more closely the phenomenon's determinism:

1) At first, only a single element of the painting present itself, a single detail of the scene (a gesture, a dress, a person's eyes, the cover of a book, the beginning of a word etc.); memories originate from a spot within a large area, at the margins of a large circle that is progressively shrinking and reducing its boundaries, its centre manifesting itself last of all. A young lady of 18, bright, quick and smart, who during these experiments had a vision of a drowned man lying on the bank of a river (an event she witnessed when she was 3 years old) told me, for instance, that the first thing she recalled was «the body of water».

2) The first detail leads, by associative concatenation, to the entire constellation of the memory. The associative processes are known to reawaken the mnemonic image from its latent state, establishing a large number of synergic neural connections and so renewing the inscriptions or engrams of the mnemonic traces.

3) The image lasts only briefly before suddenly disappearing.

4) The memory is for the most part extremely precise and clear, and often accompanied by every detail regarding that certain event and by every sensation (tactile, thermal, pain, visual, auditory, olfactory etc.) the examinee experienced for the first time in that given moment of his past. It could well be said that they do not simply remember, but relive that remote instant of time, since, in this case, the mnemonic image – contrary to the general rule – does not differ at all from the original, primary perceptive image.

5) The memory is usually localized in the early years of existence, after the age of 3 years, though occasionally it can be linked to more recent events.

6) The memory elicited by the mysterious vibration is not the same as that evoked by our will or those sudden flashes of memory which sometimes occur as a fortuitous result of mnemonic mechanisms, differentiating itself in the following ways:

a) Its sudden, almost meteoric onset;

b) A number of peculiarities and trivial details that escape common memories, but are observable with great precision here in the field of memory, characterizing this spectacle of artificial recreation;

c) The uncommon clarity of the image, despite its being fragmented.

d) The novelty of the memory, which had never before come to mind and now reappears unexpectedly, like pieces of a wreckage brought to the surface by a sudden storm after time immemorial.

e) Often accompanied by sensory experiences (auditive, taste, olfactory etc.) that are generally missing from, or, if present, are never as prominent, in common reconstructions of the past; so much so that, in this case, the memory could almost pass for a hallucination.

f) It is for us an exceptional event to be able to see ourselves in our memories as 3- or 4-year-old children, and to hear ourselves speak in the voice we had at the time, as can sometimes happen during this kind of experience.

Cutaneous areas linked to the evocation of names and numbers.

The median or axial line of the index finger of a hand (or the second toe of the foot) – which according to my current knowledge, due to its functional meaning, is like its fellows no wider than a millimetre – is in a broad sense the line of unitary memory, as it associates and assimilates within itself all other memories, though these remain distinct in accordance with Ribot's concept, and may be visual, auditive, olfactory, and so on.

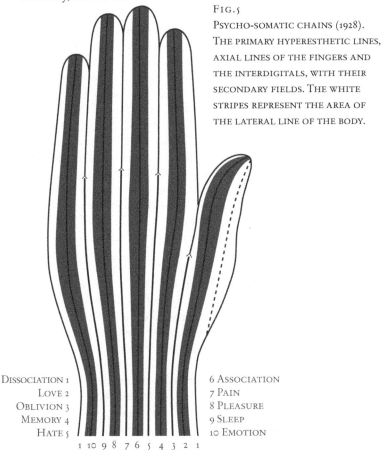

Fig. 5

Psycho-somatic chains (1928). The primary hyperesthetic lines, axial lines of the fingers and the interdigitals, with their secondary fields. The white stripes represent the area of the lateral line of the body.

Dissociation 1
Love 2
Oblivion 3
Memory 4
Hate 5

6 Association
7 Pain
8 Pleasure
9 Sleep
10 Emotion

1 10 9 8 7 6 5 4 3 2 1

This wondrous chain, laid out in the second finger of the hand and centred on its median line, can, when made to vibrate, elicit the most ancient memories of our lifetime, meaning those that were better organized and imprinted on the soft wax of the infant brain, and so doomed to sputter out following the more recent, according to a famous law of memory. It's a lightning-fast bullet moving the paleo-encephalic sphere of memory, an invisible plough working a field ploughed by Freud, and is considered representative of the *Paleo-Psyche* in general, and not only of the *Eroticum.*

But on its sides, both the left and the right, for a space of approximately 1 cm, several secondary lines run parallel to it, which we shall study in future, for they channel specialized memories, thus forming what I shall now call the cutaneous areas of memory. As we shall see, these occur in stripes, assuming a regular rectangular shape (see FIG.5) and arranged across the entire surface of the body according to fixed rules.

And so, for the purpose of initiating you to the great mysteries of nature, in this new temple of biological miracles, today I tell you that on the half of the index finger (and of the second toe of the foot) facing the thumb on the ventral face as on the dorsal, adhering to the axial line runs a thin cutaneous strip, the stimulation of which makes a cerebral connection with names (you'll find the vocabulary of names here); whilst on the other half, the one facing the middle finger, is an analogous thin strip of skin whose stimulation is linked to numbers [2].

If there were a given name, for instance, that you were simply unable to recall, you would subject the outer side of the left index to a light scratching stimulus, using the tip of the fingernail of one of the fingers of your right hand, or the nails of two fingers as though repeatedly pinching it, for 5 minutes or longer. You must enter the correct state of body and spirit required for the successful completion of the experience, which I earlier mentioned, and will in this way witness the reappearance in your memory of the mislaid name. You will apply the same manoeuvre to the inner side of the same finger [3] if you wish to recall a forgotten number (for instance a date, etc.).

Following this message sent to yourselves from a somatic station and received by the deepest storerooms of your memory, which is left rocked and shaken throughout its depots, the subconscious process of recollection takes place in four stages, as a rule. If the information to be recovered is a name, the careful examiner will, after a few minutes of charging with their thoughts cantered on that particular person, hear flow through his mind:

At first, an array of names.

Secondly, they the insistent recurrence of names beginning with the same letter as the forgotten name.

Third, the sought-after name will suddenly cross their mind for an instant, quickly vanishing before it can be seized.

Fourth and last, abruptly, automatically, after a moment of emotion, the name will jump out as though from a Jack-in-the-Box, providing a sense of satisfaction; the recollection is often linked to a fragmented view of faces, places and things relating to the person whose name we sought.

A similar process takes place when we attempt to raise a number from the sepulchre of oblivion.

I give you warning, to prevent you from encountering incidents of chance or suggestion – seemingly a ready, easy foothold for superficial criticism of my studies on the *hyperesthetic lines of the body,* but in reality already water under a bridge, an overcome hurdle, an objection refuted by twenty years of research and thousands of experiments – that in a handful of minutes, through this stimulation, more than one forgotten name may surface from the deep shadows of psychic night into the bright light of consciousness.

4. The corresponding physiognomic state is that of meditation.

5. Remote memories continue to appear for approximately fifteen minutes, as though the tremor having shaken the central depots of the subconscious had spread to its surroundings and affected neighbouring areas, generating a number of will o'the wisps in the graveyards of memory. Oftentimes the subject of the experiment has visions, for a while, of names and numbers written on the walls, and, should they continue to excite the chain, circumstances of the place and facts relating to the event may appear.

6. Nature, having placed the peacefulness of sleep close to the cerebral storm we call "emotion", and pleasure next to pain, has also assigned memory to the field next to oblivion. Charging the 1st interdigital line is enough to strangle the flow of thoughts and the exuberance of memories (hypermnesia).

7. Exciting this linear chain for 5/10/15 minutes before sleep, has the exceptional result of populating one's dreams with distant memories and remote, forgotten events, allowing them to relive the early days of their life with insurmountable clarity and unimaginable precision, for a much longer period of time than during the waking hours.

I must point out, regarding these dreams of childhood memories, that if one of these memories should present itself during the course of the day, for instance, it will again appear during the night, clearer and more detailed. I was greatly struck by the fact that this dream, which some others of a different tone, generated by the stimulation of the corresponding line, sometimes occur on two consecutive nights and repeat themselves in all their minute details. The same phenomenon may take place during waking hours, due to the effects of the charge, always recalling the same person or image.

8. There's no doubt this chain is associated with memory disorders (amnesia – paramnesia – hypermnesia – dismnesia in general – split personality). One can surmise amnesiac states may greatly benefit from stimulation of this chain.

9. It's quite likely the charging of this chain could give us a better understanding concerning the mnemonic abilities of the examinee, especially as regards their evocative memory.

THE LINEAR CHAIN OF HATE
(2ND INTERDIGITAL)

1. Feeling of being lightly touched on the lower pole of the testicle on the side being examined, and, simultaneously, on the tip of the nipple on the same side. Besides this, there is one more symptom, and that is the loss of the sense of smell on that same side *(testicular phenomenon + mammary phenomenon + ipsilateral anosmia)*.

2. Mentally, one feels the need to grit the teeth, and sometimes clench the fists. Whilst the former phenomenon manifests early, the latter is generally more delayed.

3. The examinee begins to experience feelings of rage and hostility, with a tendency to jut the jaw and the rest of the body forward, and to lunge with sudden impetus, struggling violently. Occipital headache, burning eyes and dry mouth, constant need to swallow, laboured breathing; sensation of having to twist the body and turn the eyes here and there with menacing attitude, smirk or bite, extend the hands as though to threaten or protect oneself from the object of hate and knit the eyebrows, nose flaring and eyes wide open. Occasionally facial convulsions occur, slight trembling of the body and a feeling of lightness or restlessness in the lower limbs.

Following a fit of blind rage leading the examinee to utter curses and insults, a profound feeling of hate sets in by degrees, first against their enemies, then against everyone, including their nearest and dearest, or even themselves (impulse to bite one's fingers and nails). Pale, ominous ideas form in their mind, so that the examinee believes to be frowned upon by their neighbours, who in the span of a few minutes have become to them "fake people".

4. The examinee perceives their having an angry expression, which the observer can indeed confirm.

5. For a half-hour after termination of the experience, the examinee continues to feel anger and hate against everything and everyone.

6. These hostile feelings can be quickly suppressed by charging the antipode, the axial line of the thumb (line of love).

7. During the oneiric state, dreams are agitated, full of arguments, anger and strife.

8. This chain is likely related to states of manic violence and persecutory delirium.

9. Its artificially-induced vibration will produce weak echoes in phlegmatic and apathetic subjects, and strong, quick reactions in bilious or choleric subjects.

THE LINEAR CHAIN OF PAIN
(III INTERDIGITAL)

1. The contralateral testicular phenomenon occurs, simultaneously with feeling of a light touch on the tip of the heteronymous nipple and the loss of smell on the opposite side *(testicular phenomenon + mammary phenomenon + contralateral anosmia)* – (charge in the right hemi-body, as with the line of hate. See back cover).
2. Sighing is the first warning sign of pain.
3. There follow mild blurred vision and bleak view of the outer world, urge to cry, sense of abandonment, occasionally labial tremors, melancholic thoughts and a growing feeling of sadness, desire to be near or impulse to call out to a dear person for comfort, tendency to turn the eyes upward, sobbing, moaning, feeling of a lump in the throat and heavy heart, a proneness to tearing up and, in some cases, fits of uncontrollable crying. The subject of the experiment automatically performs gestures typical of someone in pain (biting their lips, wringing their hands, etc.), clearly betraying their psychalgia and sad view of the world, which they perceive to be wrapped in a blanket of fog, the objects in it smaller than they really are. They confess to finding themselves in the condition of someone "awaiting a great disaster to befall them" or who has "already endured great suffering". "I feel like the most wretched man on earth": so a young man told me, begging me to interrupt the experiment.

Muscle contractions may occur in the face, torso and limbs, with halting breath, vasomotor disorders etc. Among the psychic disruptions to be mentioned are an unusual degree of goodwill toward everyone, a few flashes of anger or hate, some small measure of religious sentiment and a tendency to mutism.

4. The examinee can distinctly, and correctly, feel their face contort into typical expressions of sadness and sorrow.

5. A sense of sadness and discouragement that can last for varying amounts of time.

6. The sweet remedy to this bitter absinthe is represented by the charging of the median line of the 4th finger (line of pleasure), which can quickly lift the grey mists of the spirit, restores the physiognomy and bring back one's smile.

7. This is the chain of painful dreams, haunted by sad events, visions of death and funerals, and causing crying during sleep.

8. Melancholic and depressive states are generally related to disruptions taking place within the functional organization of this system.

9. Charging this hyperesthetic line is of little effect in subjects with a cheerful disposition, but greatly efficacious in those naturally predisposed to melancholy (dysthymia and depression), and as such is useful in revealing this aspect of one's temperament.

THE LINEAR CHAIN OF PLEASURE
(MEDIAN LINE OF THE RING FINGER)

1. The subject of the experiment feels a light touch on the inside of the mouth, in line with the point where lower lips and gums meet *(lower labial-gingival phenomenon)*.
2. The first sign is a smile, forming and playing on the lips.
3. After a few minutes of charging the line, the examinee feels a sense of serene calm, sweet abandon, lightheartedness, general physical wellbeing, contentedness and cheerfulness. Caught up in this paradise of somatic euphoria and earthly happiness, they begin to entertain positive thoughts, to perceive bewitching visions, harbour fond hopes, develop an unusual sense of sympathy and generosity toward everyone, compassion for their enemies, absence of worries or concerns of any kind.

They claim to feel their eyes laughing, which are in reality shining; they are under the impression of breathing in the freshness of a spring day, feel reborn and rejuvenated, feel the need to move, talk and keep themselves occupied, and are overjoyed to be alive. Refrains of cheerful songs or music from happier times come into their minds, and they feel the urge to sing, or, more commonly hum. In this joyous atmosphere, it seems to them the objects around them are larger and that the light of the surroundings is brighter. They wish to surround themselves with happy people, and sometimes feel the need to raise the head and tilt it backward, eyes uplifted, as though to revel in delight.

They laugh or smile, inflate the cheeks or dilate the nostrils, close their eyes in pleasure or open them wide with happiness, wave their arms, extend their legs or twist the torso. A sudden, strong sexual craving and desire to be caressed are not uncommon during this state of pleasure.

4. As in other cases, the examinee clearly feels that the expressions on his face reflect the sentiments of their spirit. The researcher, for his part, can see at a glance

that during this test the examinee's joy is written over their smiling lips and shining eyes.

5. The sense of euphoria continues even after the experiment ends, and then gradually fades away.

6. While this line of Nirvana gives wings to thought and acts like morphine for pain, charging the nearby interdigital line, the 3rd, is physiologically destined to abruptly sedate the euphoric exuberance and joyous expansiveness of the happy man.

7. This is the magical chain of pleasant dreams.

8. Euphoric and hypomanic states draw their flair from the source under consideration, though the association of different currents (mixed states) may occur.

9. The vibration of this chain, which may have a strong and instant or weak and delayed impacts on the humoral sphere, can reveal the circumstances of natural cheerfulness or deep-seated sadness the subject of the experiment generally navigates during the course of their life.

THE LINEAR CHAIN OF SLEEP
(IV INTERDIGITAL)

1. The examinee perceives a tightness around the root of the nose, and an instantaneous binding sensation or light touch or pain in the teeth of the upper jaw, in the precise moment the line is worked upon *(upper dental phenomenon)*.

2. Heavy eyelids *(gravedo palpebrarum)* and yawning, open or repressed, are harbingers of the experience, heralding the embrace of Morpheus.

3. After these initial signs, the rest of the sequence follows: slight dizziness accompanied by blurred vision *(vertigo obnubilans)*, confusion, light-headedness, burning eyes, occasionally tearful, to which the examinee automatically brings his hands as though to rub them or which they make an effort to widen. Feeling cold; the head falling forward; upward rotation of the eyes; slowdown of the cardiac cycle and breathing movements; confusion in ideas; growing asthenia; mental fatigue; loss of attention, reflection, memory, affection, interest for the outside world; rapidly progressive drowsiness with a tendency to assume a foetal position, or rather, the individual's favoured resting position.

4. Drowsy expression.

5. State of mental sluggishness and psychic obfuscation, of somnolentia laevis. After the experiment, some subjects may feel the need to extend the arms and stretch, like someone yawning from sleepiness.

6. Drowsiness can soon be reduced by charging the axial line of the pinkie, which, by embodying emotion, is also the line of wakefulness and cerebral storms, in contrast to oneiric peacefulness; like caffeine given as an antidote to the hypnotic potions of red poppies.

7. Charging this chain results in a deeper sleep than is natural, with dreams inhabited by *Lilliputian* visions, generally manifesting only during that period of time just before awakening.

These visions, still a mystery for psychologists and psychiatrists of our time, don't refer only to people and objects, but to the entire universe (the sky appears to hang quite low), or oftentimes to the sleeping subject themselves. Images of new-borns and children appear repeatedly within this oneiric world of dwarves.

Someone drew my attention to how easily these dreams are forgotten, only to be remembered later, and informed me that Lilliputian visions occasionally occur following charging of the 4th interdigital line, even during waking hours, if the eyes are closed.

8. This linear chain is associated with lethargy, narcolepsy, sleeping sickness etc.

9. This exam may well provide some information regarding subjects who are insomniac or hypersomniac by nature.

THE LINEAR CHAIN OF EMOTION
(MEDIAN LINE OF THE PINKIE)

1. A momentary sensation of a very light touch on the upper lip is simultaneous to the charge of the axial line of the pinkie finger *(upper lip phenomenon)*.

2. Anxiety is the first manifest effect of emotion, immediately followed by anguish.

3. Restlessness, impatience, starts of surprise and shortness of breath quickly set in on the examinee, who begins to suffer various paraesthesia, feels the need to open the eyes wide, the throat closing and the heart aching, the teeth chattering, the tongue dry and the head heavy. They are then seized with shivers, heart palpitations and vasomotor disorders; taken over by a fearful sense of expectation; claim to be afraid, to feel their legs have turned to jelly, occasionally have tears in their eyes. The time to study the emotional representations in all their stages is short, as the agitated, anxious subject will usually plead for the suspension of the experiment.

4. The corresponding physiognomic picture is typically that of a man shaken by emotion and fear.

5. A mild state of anxiety and agitation may persist for some time following the experiment, which may delay sleep if practiced in the evening hours.

6. Nature, which makes use of opposites for its own purposes, has placed peace at the side of war, and calm next to storm, for the 4th interdigital line, the line of sleep, is the sovereign soother of anxiety and emotions

7. This is the chain whose clanking chains disturb the stillness of sleep and determines the occurrence of dreams fraught with frightening moments and terrifying imagery.

8. The production mechanisms of states of anxiety, anguished neuroses and psychoneuroses are generally hidden amongst the meshes of this fatal net of human torment and distress.

9. The charging of this chain (materialized from the thyroid and steeped in adrenalin) is the touchstone for anxious states and the most sensitive reagent of emotional constitutions. Apathetic or frigid subjects provide languid, delayed responses to these appeals.

THE LINEAR CHAIN
OF MENTAL ASSOCIATION

1. The *"meatus phenomenon"* arises, as has already been described and covered numerous time in my works. It is consistent with the sensation of a light touch around the urinary opening, one of the most sensitive areas of the body, through which the median line passes. This phenomenon is accompanied by a second, momentary sensation of a longitudinal cut on the middle of the forehead, made along the path of the body's median line the instant the stimulus is applied to the latter.

2. The first symptom affecting the mind is a sense of confusion and heavy-headedness, similar to the aftermath of a traumatic head injury.

3. A heaviness falls upon the eyelids as the examinee grows progressively more confused. The mental sluggishness increases, until thoughts are muddled, hard to pin down and nebulous, disrupted due to a loosening of association; the rate of cerebration slows, mental processing becomes difficult. Concentration is reduced, perception delayed, judgement weakened; the subject is disoriented in space and time. Mild anxiety, slight dizziness, slow breathing, weak pulse, lagging speech, dry mouth, asthenia and sense of poor motility, profound depression, annihilation and depersonalization. Drowsiness, bradypsychia, bradyphasia. The examinee describes their mental state thus: "I'm dull-minded, I'm confused, I don't know how to think anymore."

If, before entering into this state, the examinee is ordered to mentally run through the alphabet, they will always falter on the same letter, and if they are asked to count, the psychic hitch will occur on the same number for each individual.

Contrary to what occurs during the charging of the lateral line of the body, the subject will feel themselves attracted instead of repulsed, preferring unity to separation and for the surrounding objects to move closer to, rather than further from, him.

4. The examinee gets the feeling of having a slow-witted face, and the observer cannot but notice they do in fact present stiff facial play, a disoriented and uncertain look that on the one hand does appear senseless, emblematic of confusion, yet on the other is contemplative, the expression of someone attempting to renew the elusive threads of their thoughts. The torso is completely unmoving, the subject's gestures have an automatic quality to them as they bring the hands up to the forehead, scratch their head, fix their hair, stroke their chin, a foot or hand twitching rhythmically. Looking into a mirror, as with every other test, the subject can, by him or herself, evaluate the changes in their physiognomy.

5. A vague sense of disorientation and mild confusion may last for some hours following the experiment, from which the subject will often attempt to remove themselves, as occurs with some of the other linear chains (those of oblivion, emotion and mental dissociation).

6. The phenomenon of mental confusion, perhaps due in this case to an overly-quick and intense summary, progressively reduces as the lateral line of the body is charged, exerting an opposite effect, since it presides over the disassociation of thought itself, as we shall soon see. Indeed, one of the most marvellous phenomena encountered during this research is the rapid change, obvious even to the subject, that takes place in their psychic personality due to the opposing charge, causing them to feel as though they were "passing over into another world".

7. This is the linear chain of confused dreams, animated by grotesque and fantastic visions, chaotic and terrible. The subject may dream of performing calculations leading to incorrect results, of making a mistake whilst counting coins, of trying and failing to recall a certain name, of trying to move and being unable to, of finding themselves in paradoxical, contradictory situations with no logical meaning, of hopelessly losing the thread without being able to give themselves an explanation of

the events, and of befuddled reasoning as confused as the subject's outer and inner world.

8. Undoubtedly, ingrained in this linear chain are mechanisms responsible for generating mental confusion. This system is associated with Meynert's Amentia.

9. It's as yet unclear on which predispositions and tendencies of human thought this linear chain might shine some light. It must be held, however, that, being interlinked with the great axial lines of the limbs and the body's median line (lines to which a special gathering and associative function is devolved), this line too must be assigned a supreme importance in thought processing and in its higher, more complicated and evolved function, that of synthesis. The links of this complicated chain, comprising within itself all other lines of body and spirit, likely give rise to sudden flashes of inspiration.

THE LINEAR CHAIN
OF MENTAL DISSOCIATION
(LATERAL LINE OF THE BODY)

1. The first physical symptom is a decline in eyesight the instant the line is excited *(ocular phenomenon)*.
2. The first sign of thought dissociation is the sudden emergence within the spirit world of a bizarre idea.
3. Gradually progressing psychic breakdown: words heard seem dragged out, distant, monotonous, truncated, stressed and sequenced like a musical rhythm.

The wall opposite is seen spotted with shadows, the bars appear divided into several parts, surrounding objects look far apart from one another, separate from their supporting surface, as though afloat in the air.

If the examinee is asked to observe one of their upper limbs, bare and extended, they describe it as being divided into two parts by a black stripe, almost as if the hand were disconnected from the arm. It becomes impossible for them to imagine two persons or objects attached; bright lights and nearby objects are a source of indescribable discomfort; proximity, unity and continuity are abhorred; there is pleasure at the sight of partition and subdivision [4]; lastly, hope is fostered that the limbs will detach from the body, and sometimes the mind holds visions or a strong sensation of dismemberment *(schizosomia)*. It often happens they can feel the eyeballs diverging, moving away from one another and dilating, like the mouth, until the cheeks almost disappear. When the eyes are closed, and later also when open, the subject thinks to see other people's arms lengthening, believing them to be mutilated and dismembered due to being able to see only the head, or a leg, or a hand.

Upon picturing the sea, the examinee sees it divided by a thin strip of land; if they imagine a large square or an extensive moor, a high wall or a vast canvas, they see them all divided by great grey or black stripes. Besides continuity, they also fear enclosure: closed doors fuel discomfort.

Should they wish to recall any text to their mind's eye, they will be able to picture the first and last lines, but not the intermediate section. Even printed words appear disjointed, the rows/lines heavily spaced; when mentally reciting a poem, a prayer etc., elisions, insertion of additional words, or transpositions may occur. During an experiment, one subject pointed out that his attempts to speak, for instance, the words *"I want to go home"* resulted in them being rendered in reverse order: *""I want home to go"*. A second examinee, after about 40 minutes' charge, heard the endophasic murmur *"I want to Attilio write"* in his head each time he tried to say *"I want to write to Attilio"*. It is extremely important to note that, during these tests, the subject is tormented by doubt and uncertainty (see psychasthenic states).

Writing tests, which I have introduced only recently and which will be easy to repeat and define, show that the pseudo-demented subject created by the experiment widens words, elides syllables, and has uncommonly large calligraphy (macrography) and an inclination to scribble odd drawings.

It's also worth noting that the strange, harrowing phenomenon of general thought dissociation and inconsistency between effects and actions, running through his mind, is clearly felt by the examinee.

4. The corresponding physiognomic picture reflects the inconsistency and bizarreness of thoughts, and the face is contorted with ever-changing grimaces, whilst remaining inexpressive during moments of rest.

5. The prominent role of this psycho-somatic chain in the organization, or disorganization of psychic personality, is also demonstrated by the seriousness and duration of the aftereffects. Indeed, following a lengthy charge of 30 or 40 minutes, the incoherency of thought and asininity in the demeanour persist, to a lesser degree, for many hours.

6. There is no shadow of doubt that the *vis medicatrix* of psychic dissociation, governed by this fundamental chain, is located in the axial line of the middle finger, which possesses the ability to perform the miracle of mental synthesis.

One should also keep in mind the fact that, following the charge of this line or of the median line of the third finger, all aforementioned phenomena can only occur in a stunted, uncertain way, since, in the first case, thoughts remain muddled, and in the second, disorganized.

7. This is the terrifying chain of mutilated dreams, the strangest, most paradoxical and incoherent to ever

haunt the phantasmagorical world of sleepers, who in their dreams see fragmented oceans and mountains, dismembered bodies, decapitated heads, detached eyeballs and straying hands, like a tumult of hellish carnage or something out of an Edgar Allan Poe tale.

By some miracle of metamorphosis and reincarnation, from this cluster of body parts a new composition of persons known to the subject can sometimes slowly take shape, fragment by fragment.

Furniture appears to have been rearranged and split into separate parts, objects are in pieces. A chair is cut in half, an armchair stands without feet. If the subject dreams of holding a pack of cards, he will notice they are incomplete, half-drawn, fragmented, and see them slipping from his hands as though attracted by a mysterious force. If they dream of wearing clothes, these detach themselves from the body, and people approach to steal them. If they dream of writing, they see the pen hovering over the paper, unable to make contact [5].

For the length of this tragicomedy, precisely recreating all the characteristics of dissociation of human thought, the subject reports discomfort about their inability to explain the strange phenomena taking place, and feel they might have "gone mad".

8.   I can assure you that the classic symptoms of schizophrenia, starting with catatonia, negativism, mannerisms and stereotypes, following with grimaces and tics, rigid, statuary attitude, vague smile, soliloquy, whispering, gesticulating, grotesque expressions, verbigeration and perseveration, and ending with psychic impediments, childishness, Forel's Wortsalat, impulses, states of excitement, delusional ideas and so on, are simple to artificially recreate in miniature by charging – for a half-hour or more – any transversal or longitudinal intermediate line, headed by the system's fundamental one, more precisely the lateral line of the body, as already outlined, highlighted and studied by me for many years.

I can also assure you that the mysterious chain of this great line of dismemberment, disconnection, dissociation and disaggregation holds within it all the tormented secrets of human madness, or *Dementia Praecox* (the word *schizophrenia*, coined by Bleuler, is perfect, revealing and irreplaceable).

❊❊❊

Gentlemen, please understand that producing these delicate phenomena, in some cases barely noticeable and almost imperceptible, is not as easy and immediate as you might think after hearing my descriptions of them, which camouflage the difficulties instead of highlighting them, emphasizing their wondrousness rather than containing them within that severity usually applied to scientific revelations. I can safely say these facts are indeed real, and that with the backing of my teachings, and of your patience, you will succeed in replicating them yourselves. Of course, if the identification of this occult web were the easiest, the simplest and most natural accomplishment on Earth, you surely agree it would have been discovered long before me by one of the countless researchers who have, over the course of time, studied man's skin sensitivity.

Don't be too surprised by the geometry I have presented to you, reproduced on the surface of our body, for in the mineral kingdom as in the vegetable and animal, Nature has given us many important geometry lessons, as well as other teachings on harmony.

Nor is it surprising that on the surface of our hand are laid out the essential passions of the heart and the opposite energies of life, and likewise the fundamental engine of human thought. Gentlemen, don't forget that within the hand there already exist, as you well know, many similar mechanisms of competition and antagonism presiding over the muscle's mechanics and the various innervations. It is we who here claim to find there fundamental differences and irreconcilable inequalities: for Nature, there is no difference between, for example, the mechanism governing the flexion and extension of the hand by means of opposite but regulated currents, and that pulling the strings of pain, hidden away inside the 3rd interdigital space, or those of pleasure, set out in the 4th finger.

However it may be, these are the facts now constituting the latest results of my research and which, I am certain, tomorrow, will achieve scientific recognition, at least in their fundamental details.

Once we will have traced and marked one of these great fundamental squares upon any area of man's body surface, with its 1st order and 2nd order lines that I am now studying and which fill the gaps of all the *small fundamental squares* (see FIG.1), each one of which must be traced in the likeness of the larger one (see FIG.4), then we shall be able to reproduce, or rather mass-produce, in the hubs of infinite linear associations and combinations, all the feelings the human brain is capable of generating, by knowingly striking special lines and *specific meeting points* with our stimuli, just as a painter achieves every colour under the sun by mixing the fundamental ones on his easel; or as a typographer prints the greatest books using individual letters; or as a pianist composes infinite sounds of the most beautiful music with the notes of their harpsichord.

What a splendid spectacle the psychologists of tomorrow will witness, when they see countless combinations (that I have already glimpsed) of the different mental images, or *nuances* of the spirit, take shape as though by magic following the excitement of the meeting points of transversal and longitudinal 1st and 2nd order lines. For instance, in one of my hypersensitive patients, suffering from multiple sclerosis, by striking the meeting point between the longitudinal line of memory and the transversal line of pleasure, then of pain, and finally of love, located in the palm of the right hand, I elicited respectively a pleasant, a painful, and lastly a *loving memory* (see Fig.6)

How wonderful! The thoughts of Homo Sapiens, a believer in free will, governed and guided by the whim of a mere pin skimming the skin of the body! The ancient Scholars were right after all when they maintained that the human soul is in every part of the body: *"Anima umana-"* they stated, *"est tota in toto corpora et in qualibet eiusparte"* (*"The human soul exists in the whole body and in each of its parts"*).

At this point, I must conclude. Allow me though, before ending, to once again to reiterate my views regarding a few fundamental issues, intimately linked to the mystery of these somatopsychic chains, by stating as follows:

1. There are many, and in my view valid, reasons why we are led to believe that these special systems of somatopsychic chains, which I consider to be simple, peculiar expressions of F.H. Lewy's *Vitalreihenketten,* entertain intimate relations with the neuro-vegetative system which to us is certainly no less than the Promised Land.

2. It's to be believed that these linear chains, which, with their opposite currents and antagonistic effects, cannot but bring to mind the corresponding games of the sympathetic and vagal systems, are in a forced, regulated and predestined relationship not only with the exocrine glands, but also with the endocrine, which are much more important to us.

3. I can already tell you that each of these chains is connected, mainly or exclusively, through its rings, to an organ of our body. With some reservation, I warn you, for instance, that the median of the thumb (and likewise of the big toe) is linked to the intestine, as the 1st interdigital is linked to the stomach; that the median of the index finger relates to the genitals and bladder, and the 2nd interdigital to the liver (and hence the temperament is referred to as bilious); that the axial of the middle finger is associated with the kidneys, and the 3rd interdigital with the spleen (English spleen days refer); that the median line of the ring finger is aligned with the pancreas, and the 4th interdigital with the lungs. The median line of the pinkie is undoubtedly the line of the heart, and the lateral of the body is likely the line of the brain.

It is a question here, gentlemen, of as many reversed chains or Head zones [6].

4. It is likely that these peripheral mechanisms find similar devices within the functional organization of nerve centres, and contain the secret of the pressing problem regarding cerebral locations. From what we've learned during the exploration of this new world, we can perhaps deduce that the so-called *nerve centres* are represented by as many nervous systems.

5. These laws we are discussing, responsible for regulating the inter-metameric correspondence and junctions of the linear systems present on the surface of the body, can probably shed light on the analogous rules governing the mechanism of the various innervations, which, in the same way, are likely to be *pluri-segmented.*

6. It is to be hoped that these phenomena of somatopsychic consequences may clarify the uncertain mechanism of hallucinations.

7. I can tell you that each of these five axial digital lines and of the four interdigital lines is the supreme ruler and overall collector of the entire phenomenal cohort I have described, including both physical and psychological repercussions, but it is not the only one affecting each set of phenomena. To the left and right of the median

and interdigital lines of each finger, covering a space of approximately 5 mm, are strips of skin depositary, with their tiny rings of secondary chains, of every difference and specialty specific to the general purpose of that particular linear chain (see Fig.5).

Thus, for example, running next to the primary line of love are the secondary lines of particular love (towards family, towards one's homeland, towards science etc.); similarly, along the primary line of oblivion run the secondary lines of systematic amnesias (visual, auditory etc.). Next to the primary line of memory pass the secondary lines of the various memories (visual, auditory, olfactory, of names, of numbers etc.); likewise, the primary line of hate is generally accompanied by the secondary lines of the particular forms of hate, even those directed towards specific people. The great miracle of the *axial line of the middle finger*, that presides over the general synthesis of thought, comprises all the lesser miracles of the nearby secondary lines responsible for the special, systematized syntheses of the spirit; and the spectacle of the *lateral line of the body*, namely the line governing general dissociation of thought, encompasses within itself all minor spectacles of its satellite secondary lines, delegated to special dissociations, to particular disorganization, to the systematic breakdown of mental operations.

Generally, the secondary lines of the various and, unfortunately, countless particular pains, be they physical, concerning one's body, or moral, concerning the individual's relationship to the outside world or to the inner world of their own soul, can be found in the vicinity of the main line of pain; the same is true for the line of pleasure (for example, I have found that in some subjects the points of pleasure of appetite, flowers, songs and music etc.) and of emotion (on one side of the smallest finger the sad emotions are represented, on the other the pleasant emotions). In this respect, one must keep in mind the fact that each individual does not have written on his skin the lists of romances, enemies, pleasures, sorrows and emotions already catalogued in essays on passions' physiology, but rather those tendencies, special affections and particular feelings intrinsically dominant within them. Therefore, each individual reacts to the excitement of these preformed chains, as to the circumstances of the outside world, according on their type.

8. Know that the primary chains of principal passions (pleasure and pain, hate and love are still the great op-

posite poles of human beings' vital currents) and of the fundamental mental processes, together with their retinue of secondary lines of operating specifications, are not present solely on the one hand, that is, they are not the domain of this new chiromancy, but can be found, in their longitudinal and transversal series, upon the entire surface of the body, at regular intervals and according to established laws.

9. It follows from the above that what we glimpsed some time ago has now certainly been proved: that specific motor impairments, having their roots in the world of neurology and organicity, determine the elective consequences to the world of psychology and functionality. As a result, it is necessary to "neurologize" psychiatry.

10. The mechanistic concept of life is confirmed, in my opinion, by the above, as are, to their very foundations, the studies on "Reflexology" by Vladimir Bechterew, who is now lost to us but in death better known than before.

On the basis of all we have seen and glimpsed, we are permitted to believe that each of these great, fundamental and primary lines, having deep roots in phylogeny and ontogeny, constitutes a solid block and has multiple representations, that is, it encompasses within its organizational structure, a specific component of all organic functions. Each one of these vital cords is, for instance, connected by one thread to sensitivity and by another to mobility (voluntary and involuntary).

Each vital chain is, for example, tied through one of its rings to splanchnology, through another to endocrinology, and so on. Lastly, every one of these unitary systems possesses an invisible silver thread to govern affection, and an obscure gold thread with which to guide man's thoughts. [7].

Gentlemen, let us not get ahead of ourselves. Today, I have disassembled a number of devices of the human "machine" that had, until now, remained hidden, within the magical chessboard of your enclosed body and the sealed mosaic of your open hand.

Meanwhile, I give you good tidings: for the Neurology and Psychiatry, Psychology and Physiology of man, a great road has been paved, leading to splendour, a new path laid open, full of marvels.

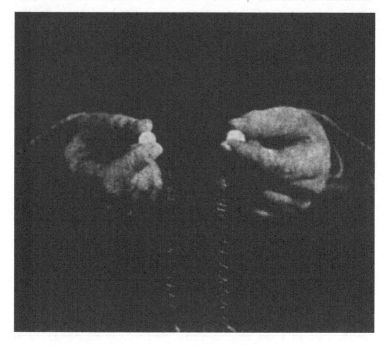

FIG.6

A LOVING MEMORY. THE SUBJECT, SITTING QUIETLY IN A MOMENT OF PEACE AND REST, HOLDS BETWEEN THE FIRST TWO FINGERS OF HIS HANDS A SMALL SPHERICAL ELECTRODE, CHARGED BY A FARADAIC CURRENT, PERCEPTIBLE BUT NOT PAINFUL. AFTER APPROXIMATELY 5-10 MINUTES, SUDDENLY AND UNBIDDEN, VIVID AND THROBBING, THERE COMES INTO HIS MIND A LONG AGO LOVING MEMORY.

NOTE

(1) See Calligaris, Research on the hyperesthetic lines of the body (6th series). (Journal of Neural and Mental Pathology) – file 5-6, 1924.

(2) In addition to numbers, this thin paramedian strip of skin on the inner part of the index finger (see Fig.5) has a relationship with geometric images.

(3) Excluding from the charging, in this case as in the first, its lateral face (represented in white in Fig.5), which is in the domain of the lateral line of the body (interdigital band), because even if it were struck by the stimulus, the memory would be hampered, being dissociated (see further on).

(4) This important phenomenon of special mental sympathies and antipathies does not only take place for the median and lateral lines, but for every other hyperesthetic line of the body. By charging the line of hate, for example, the subject will abhor all thoughts of love; and by charging the line of pain, every pleasant image will be disagreeable to them. Placing before him irregular and deformed objects on the one side and regular, geometrical objects on the other, following a few minutes' "charge" (electrical or mechanical) of the cutaneous field of numbers and geometrical images, located, as we said, in the inner paramedian area of the second finger (see back), they will report dislike for the former and sympathy or attraction for the latter, showing a predilection for order, that is for the rule, and an aversion for disorder, whilst contemplating the objects around them, which he is almost induced to count and numerically multiply.

(5) Following the charge of the median line, objects, in dreams, often appear close and piled together.

(6) Lately, I have established the existence of antidromic currents along the pathways considered herein, that is, I have been able to prove, through experimentation,

that the phenomena are reversible, since each of these preformed somato-psychic chains has a corresponding psycho-somatic chain. Indeed, I have found that:

a) not only does the stimulation of one of these special lines have an elective impact on the psychic realm, arousing different feelings (love, hate, pain, pleasure etc.), but that the primitive mental representation, in turn, affects the somatic realm, more precisely, the cutaneous fields I have indicated, represented by intersecting longitudinal and transversal strips (see FIG.5), prearranged and unchangeable *(psycho-cutaneous reflex)*.

b) not only does the stimulation of these particular lines have an elective impact upon a given organ (heart, lungs, stomach, intestine, liver etc.), but the primitive mental representation of a state of mind (loving, hateful, painful, pleasant etc.) also affects the body, arousing aches, paraesthesia, hyper kinesis etc. in that specific organ which, according to the rule I indicated, has ties to that specific linear chain *(psycho-splanchnic reflex)*;

c) Lastly, I think it likely that the illness of a given organ, too, as it causes upon the skin a hyperalgesic area of Head, on the one hand disturbs, as we already know, the sensitivity of the skin, (as regards the hand, see FIG. 5) in the dominion of its special chain (splanchno-cutaneous reflex), and, on the other hand, as is also known to us, confers its own particular hue to the spirit world *(splanchno-psychic reflex)*.

The diagnostics for internal illnesses may therefore have new light shed on it by these findings, and I entrust the urgent problem to the wisdom and patient investigations of our clinicians.

(7) Finally, I wish to mention four experiments, of great ease and simplicity, to any amateur researcher hoping to quickly arrive at that clear view and precise understanding of the phenomena which I only succeeded in reaching, lento pede, after twenty years' work.

I. As regards the *somato-psychic linear chains,* let them encourage 10 or 100 subjects from a college, military barracks or hospital – who must be unaware of the value of these mysterious lines- to "charge" a given axial line of the fingers or interdigital line of the left hand, exciting it crosswise, with the tip of the nail of the right-side index or middle finger, for 10/15 minutes, in the evening, before sleep (see back).

The next day, let the researcher take the account of the subjects' dreams, and they shall see them to be the truest, most certain and infallible witnesses of the functional meaning of these ancient and indestructible chains connecting man's body to his spirit *(cutaneo-oneiric reflex)*.

II. A subject sitting quietly, in a moment of peace and rest, holds between the last phalanx of the thumb and index fingers of each (damp) hand a small spherical electrode, soaked in warm water and charged by a Faradic current of moderate intensity (FIG. 6). The researcher assisting will facilitate the test by briefly increasing the current's intensity for a few moments, in surges, imparting light, quick shocks to the electrical device's shoe.

After a variable period of time (5/15 minutes), the examinee, who must be in a state of Buddhist quiet, his mind devoid of thought, will feel suddenly startled, having seen unfold before their mind's eye, sudden and unexpected, a *distant memory of love.*

This will generally consist of an episode of sexual love, but occasionally the memory will be more sacred than profane, having ties to familial love (paternal, maternal, fraternal, filial), and even more seldom to patriotic love, or humanitarian, etc. The latter case occurs in two situations: a) when the examinee is young, under twenty years old, and as such the evoked memory, which is, as a rule, very distant (see back) cannot be joined to sexual affections that would have been far too premature in childhood or adolescence – b) when the examinee, despite being older, holds the two electrodes, not in conjunction with the axial or median lines of the thumbs *(primeval line of sexual love)*, but over the nearby areas *(cutaneous fields of love in the broad sense)*, where the different types of specialized, extra-sexual loves of human beings are represented.

It so happened, for example, that this experience elicited this forgotten memory in a girl of 20 years, who, when she was 6 years old, in a show of filial affection, ran into her father's arms; whilst a 37-year-old woman suddenly recalled being lovingly rocked in her mother's arms, in an extremely distant moment of her early child-hood, when she was not yet 3 years old, going as far as to remember seeing, through her small, innocent, upturned eyes, the image of her mother's loose blonde hair.

III. As concerns the corresponding psycho-somatic chains that have recently made their way into our investigations, in order to bring forth incontrovertible proof, the researcher will ask the subject to immerse their hands in warm water, and will then apply an electrode to one, leaving the other free for the *experimentum crucis*, the crucial experiment.

The examinee will then be asked, following a few minutes' reflection, to willingly create in his mind a given representation (of love, pain, pleasure, pain etc.), as natural and vivid as possible.

Now, when the researcher starts moving the dampened electrode, alive with a mild Faradic current, transversally across the palm of the hand in question, the instant it makes contact with the band of skin shown in FIG.5, corresponding to that feeling that has been artificially elicited, the subject will experience two symptoms:

a) A hypo-, or more often a hyperaesthesia upon the (digital or interdigital) strip of skin, which, in accordance with my chart, corresponds to the nature of the mental representation *(body's response: psycho-cutaneous reflex);*

b) Instantaneous intensification of the psychic representation taking place *(spirit's response: cutaneo-psychic reflex).*

IV. In recent days, I have noticed that superficial "charges" (mechanical, electrical etc.) of hyperesthetic lines, when occurring in slow succession (approximately around 60/90 in one minute, as mentioned above), stimulate the line's function, whereas when livelier and swifter (about 200 per minute) the effect is opposite, paralyzing the line's function.

Indeed, with this last method it is possible to artificially create – as I will explain in other studies – not only a special *sensory-motor paralysis,* but an elective *psychic paralysis.* In other words, if this rapid stimulation is applied by means of a metal point, the tip of a finger-nail (fingernail test) or an electrode charged with a Faradic current so intense as to be only just bearable, transversally across a longitudinal line on the palm of the hand, for instance, after a few minutes the psychic function belonging to that line will be inhibited. If, for example, such a rough, quick stimulation were applied to the palm of the hand (upon an area no larger than 1 cm, so as to prevent the charge of the neighbouring longitudinal lines) across the path of the 2nd interdigital (line of hate), not only will it be impossible to elicit any feelings of anger or hate in the examinee, as is the case when stimulation is slow and brief (see back), but it will be absolutely impossible for the subject to even form a hateful thought, or imagine a hateful sentiment directed towards anyone.

BIBLIOGRAPHY
OF Giuseppe CALLIGARIS

Calligaris, Giuseppe: *Il pensiero che guarisce,*
Udine, 1901 (Doktorarbeit)

Calligaris, Giuseppe: *Un medico e la guerra,*
Ferrara, 1922 (Casa Editrice Taddei)

Calligaris, Giuseppe: *Le catene lineari del corpo e dello spirito,*
Udine 1928 (Tipografia Doretti)

Calligaris, Giuseppe: *Le catene lineari secondarie del corpo
d dello spirito,* Rom, 1930 (Casa Editrice Pozzi)

Calligaris, Giuseppe: *La fabbrica dei sentimenti sul corpo dell´uomo,*
Rom, 1932 (Casa Editrice Pozzi)

Calligaris, Giuseppe: *Le meraviglie dell´autoscopia,*
Rom, 1933 (Casa Editrice Pozzi)

Calligaris, Giuseppe: *Le meraviglie dell´eterscopia,*
Rom, 1934 (Casa Editrice Pozzi)

Calligaris, Giuseppe: *Telepatia e radio-onde cerebrali,*
Mailand, 1934 (Hoepli)

Calligaris, Giuseppe: *Telepatia e telediagnosi,*
Udine, 1935 (Istituto Edizioni Accademiche)

Calligaris, Giuseppe: *Le immagine del vivi e dei morti richiamati
dalle loro opere,* Udine, 1935 (Istituto Edizioni Accademiche)

Calligaris, Giuseppe: *L´universo rappresentato sul corpo dell´uomo,*
Udine, 1937 (Istituto Edizioni Accademiche)

Calligaris, Giuseppe: *Il cancro,*
Udine, 1937 (Istituto Edizioni Accademiche)

Calligaris, Giuseppe: *Malattie infettive,*
Udine, 1938, (Istituto Edizioni Accademiche)

Calligaris, Giuseppe: *Le meraviglie del corpo umano,*
Udine, 1938 (Istituto Edizioni Accademiche)

Calligaris, Giuseppe: *Le meraviglie della Metapsichica,*
Mailand, 1940 (F. Ili Boca)

Calligaris, Giuseppe: *Nuove ricerche sul cancro,*
Mailand, 1940 (F. Ili Boca)

Calligaris, Giuseppe: *Malattie mentali,*
Mailand, 1940 (F. Ili Boca)

Calligaris, Giuseppe: *Deliquenza malattia mentale,*
Brest, 1942 (Casa Editrice Vannini)

Calligaris, Giuseppe: *La luna,*
Brest, 1942 (Casa Editrice Vannini)

Calligaris, Giuseppe: *Le meraviglie della Metafisiologia,*
Brest, 1944 (Casa Editrice Vannini)

Since you ate the apple from the tree of ignorance,
you have thrown yourself out of paradise.
Being free of physical food is your primordial state.

The
YOGA
of Breatharianism

Joachim M. Werdin
Abuna Semai

Your fear tried to cut demons off their God-given existance.
y this you share their fate: been disconnected to the True Home.
To reenter, face them with all your unconditional Love.

Stefan Strecker

All my beloved demons

Sunmeditation

"Through gazing into the sun,
one creates the body of a buddha...
in which all impure or conditioned elements
dissolve into five-coloured rainbow light
or subtle illusory body."

The 14th Dalai Lama

www.sunmeditation.info

Made in the USA
Las Vegas, NV
10 March 2021